FULL MOON
SURVIVOR

ANDREA FAHSELT

FULL MOON SURVIVOR
Copyright © 2024 by Andrea Fashelt

ISBN: 978-1639458462 (sc)
ISBN: 978-1639458479 (e)

All rights reserved. No part of this publication may be reproduced, distributed, or transmitted in any form or by any means, including photocopying, recording, or other electronic or mechanical methods, without the prior written permission of the publisher and/or the author, except in the case of brief quotations embodied in critical reviews and other noncommercial uses permitted by copyright law.

The views expressed in this book are solely those of the author and do not necessarily reflect the views of the publisher, and the publisher hereby disclaims any responsibility for them.

Writers' Branding
(877) 608-6550
www.writersbranding.com
media@writersbranding.com

WHEN I ARISE FROM THE FLAMES

I WILL HAVE FASHIONED WINGS FROM ASHES

TOSSED COINS

WITHERED LASHES

I WILL CHANGE RAGE TO LOVE

WHITE AS A DOVE

STEP OUT OF THE FIRE

WHITE AS LIGHT

HE THREW HIS SWORD IN THE OCEAN

WASHED HIS HANDS CLEAN

NO ONE WOULD BELIEVE THE MYSTERIES HE HAD SEEN

LOCKED AND GUARDED

ANGRY AND SCARED

IT WAS A LIFE OF SOLITUDE

EXILE AND PAIN OF GREAT MAGNITUDE

ALL YOU NEED TO KNOW

IS I FELL ASLEEP WATCHING YOU SMILE

MY CONCENTRATION DEEP

IT TOOK A WHILE

I DIDNT WANT TO MISS A MINUTE

DRIFTING IN AND OUT OF CONSCIOUSNESS

AFRAID OF ANY OF YOU I MIGHT MISS

JUDGING EYES

JUDGING LIES

I STARE OUT TO WHERE THE ARMS REACH FAR

WHAT IS THE FAIR CALL

FINGERS CROOKED LIKE WILTED BRANCHES IN THE FALL

HOLDS MY JUDGEMENT TO WASH MY BODY OF THIS DISCONTENT

OUT PAST THE HORIZON

FOG AND BITTER SCENT

I WISH FOR THE TIME TO SEND ME BACK

BACK TO WHERE I WAS MEANT

PRIDE REGAL AS A LION FACE

JEWELS FOR EYES

YOUR SEEKING DARKNESS SETS PACE

LIKE A WEEPING PHANTOM

IN THE NIGHT,THEY DO COME

DEFINING YOUR WORTH BY A COIN,TATTERED GARB

SPECTER SHADOW,PITCH HUE OF MUD

IT'S CHEECKS SO SALLOW

EYES COLOUR OF BLOOD

LOOK OF DISGRACE

LOOKING AT MY FACE

IT IS SOMETHING YOU SHOULD KNOW

I HIDE DISAPPOINTED

MISERY IS MY WHOA

DON'T TALK TO ME OF LESSONS

DRAWN OUT IN LINES OF LYRICS

IT IS SOMETHING YOU SHOULD KNOW

MISTAKEN KINDNESS FOR WEAKNESS

ECHOED ON THE WINDS THAT BLOW

CASTING SHADOWS ACROSS THE WATER

GLARING LIGHT THROUGH WINDOWS

IT IS SOMETHING YOU SHOULD KNOW

BROKEN MUSIC BOX OF BONES
MY CLOSET FULL OF GHOSTS CRY AND MOAN
PAPER DOLLS CHANTING IN THE RAIN
THE LONESOME BALLERINA WILL NEVER BE THE SAME
WONDER IF I CLOSE MY EYES
IF I CAN FACE THE DARKNESS UNKNOWN
RIPPED LACE TOO PRECIOUS TO BE SEWN
LOST..BROKEN..FIGHT TO GET HOME
GIVE BACK TO ME ONCE TREASURED PAST
THE FAMILIAR SCENT OF A LIT MATCH
WAVES THAT LEAP IN DREAMS THAT CREEP
FROM ONCE MY TATTERED BED
MY SOMBER STRENGHT
I CAN NOT SLEEP

COME..

BE WITH ME AND BE MY LOVE..

I'LL MAKE A DRESS OF BRIGHT CRIMSON ROSES

AND DANCE WITH THEE IN ELEGANT POSES

COME..

BE WITH ME AND BE MY LOVE..

I'LL MAKE SHELTER FOR YOU FROM THE RAIN

WASH AWAY ALL THE PAIN

COME..

BE WITH ME AND BE MY LOVE..

I'LL SCRIPT MAGIC INTO POETRY

VERSE AS LONG AND AS FREE

IT WAS AT FIRST LIGHT

YOU CAME CRASHING INTO ME

YOUR RAGE.. YOUR FURY

FREE SPIRT.. THE ONLY THING YOU KNEW HOW TO BE

YOU'D DISAPPEAR THEN REAPPEAR

FEELING OF EMPTINESS AND LOSS

YOU MADE ME SEE EMPATHY FROM YOUR EYES

AND THE MILLION NIGHTS I'D AGONIZE

HOPING TO BEG FOR YOUR AFFECTIONS

YOUR DISCRIMINATORY ATTENTION

IT CAME AT FIRST LIGHT

MY FIRST INTERNAL FIGHT

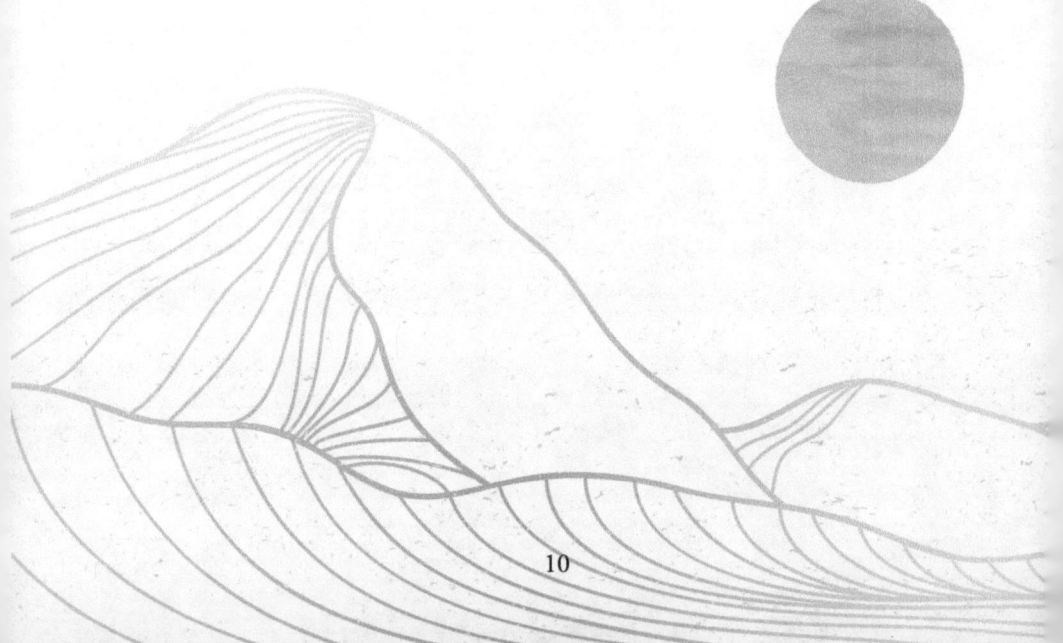

LOST SIGHT FOR A MOMENT

CAUGHT GLIMPSE IN THE WET DROP

AND THE SMELL OF THE RAIN THAT DAY

I WAS REMINDED OF YOU

OF ALL YOU GAVE

THE SUNSET BEHIND THE TREES

LOST SIGHT FOR A MOMENT

OF WHAT IS IMPORTANT

ALLOWING MYSELF TO ENJOY ONE SMALL PIECE OF LIGHT

LOST SIGHT AND FELT UNWORTHY OF GOOD

UNTIL I SAW YOUR SMILE

KNOWING IT WAS BECAUSE OF ME

LET'S GO WHERE THE TREES BREATH THE WIND

WHERE THE SILENCE IS SOUND

LET'S GO..

WHERE OUR HEARTS ARE PURE

AND RADIATE LIGHT FROM OUR SOULS

LET'S GO WHERE THE SNOW FALLS IN

TUNES OF A LULLABY SOFT ON THE GROUND

LET'S GO..

TO WHERE YOU WHISPER MY NAME

AND I AM SURROUNDED IN LUSTER OF GOLD

LET'S GO..

WHERE DUSK WRITES OUR NEXT MOVE

WHERE WE SEE OUR PAST

OUR PRESENT ..OUR FUTURE

DRAWN ACROSS THE DARK SKY

LET'S GO...

IT'S THE EARTH THAT SINGS YOUR PRAISES

IT CHANGES BUT SOMEHOW EACH SEASON IT FEELS THE SAME

LOVE..LIFE..LAST BREATH

I CAN HEAR IT ECHO IN THE WIND

THE CHANGING OF THE TIDE

FEELS FAMILIAR EACH TIME

YOU RISE..

ALWAYS WONDERING...

THIS CHANGE..

YOUR HEART SEES AND FEELS THE SAME

LIVE..LIFE.. LAST BREATH

WE WALK THIS LINE TOGETHER

EACH DAY..EACH YEAR..IN LOVE

IN CHANGE..LAST BREATH

THROW ME TO THE WOLVES

AND I SHALL RETURN WITH TAME CREATURE BY MY SIDE

I LIVE BLINDLY IN A WAR WITHIN MY MIND

CUT ME OUT..LIKE A DISEASE

POISONING YOUR BODY

BUT I SHALL RETURN OF HEALTHY SOUL

WE WEAR BLINDFOLDS TO NAVIGATE THE ROAD

NEVER FORGIVING MISTAKES

THROW ME INTO THE FIRE

AND I SHALL RETURN WITH GOLDEN EMBERS IN MY EYES

LOCKED IN FURY OF MY JOURNEY

ONE DAY I'LL FORGET I LOVED YOU

FORGET ALONG THE WAY

HOW I OCCUPIED MY MIND WITH

ANGST..TORTURE..ANGUISH

IT WILL FADE

REPLACED WITH A DISTANT MEMORY OF THE CONSTANT POUNDING

POUNDING OF MY CHEST

SEARING HEAT

LONGING ACHE

ONE DAY I'LL FORGET I LOVED YOU

STRIP THE VISIONS OF HAUNTING EXPRESSIONS OF WHAT WAS PLAYING OVER

REWINDING IN THE BACK OF MY MIND

ONE DAY I'LL FORGET I LOVED YOU

ROSES IN MY HANDS

RIPPED JEANS

BRUISES ON BOTH KNEES

LOOKING AT YOU THROUGH BLACK EYES

A GUARDED STARE MY DISGUISE

IT MUST OF BEEN DARK

HIGH UP

SO IT SEEMS

IT MUST OF BEEN LONELY

WHERE NOONE HEARS YOUR SCREAMS

IT MUST OF BEEN A PUNISHMENT

OF YOUR DISCONTENTMENT

STRAPPED DOWN IN THE PITS OF A CRADLE

CRACKED AND UNSTABLE

ROSES IN MY HANDS

RIPPED JEANS

BRUISES ON BOTH KNEES

LOOKING AT YOU THROUGH BLACK EYES

MY GUARDED STARE BECOMES YOUR HYPNOTISE

PULLED THE VEIL OFF AND REVEALED NATURE'S MASK

EARTH PROTECTING IT'S FACE

FOR ONE TIME WE LISTENED

TIME WASTED ON DEAF EAR

LOOK TO THE SOUND OF WIND CALLING

OF HUMANITY FALLING

SHORE HIGH OF FEAR

PULLED THE VEIL OFF AND REVEALVED NATURE'S INTENT

FIND SOLACE IN THE MESSAGE NATURE SENT

DID WE FORGET ABOUT THE SEASON

DAWN OF A NEW DAY

THIS WILL NOT BE THE DEMISE THAT WASHES US AWAY

WIPE OUR EYES

DIG DEEP BENEATH OUR FEARS

WE LISTEN FOR BOARDED GATES TO COLLAPSE

BUT WITHOUT OUR EARS

THEY WALK IN CAPES AND CLOAKS

ARMOUR MADE OF TIN

FASHIONED BY THE FIRE BURNING WITHIN

WAS YOUR INTENT TO SET MY SOUL ON FIRE

WATCH IT BURN.. CLAIM ASHES WITH SUCH DESIRE

EMBERS BRIGHT SMOLDERING LIGHT

IT WAS WITHOUT A MATCH ..A SPARK

YOU LEFT ME BURNING IN THE DARK

AFTER THE SAND FILLED IN WE EMERGE FROM ROTTING SOIL
THE CRACKS OF DECAYED BONES
WIPED OUR EYES FROM UNLIT TOMBSTONES
VICTIMS OF EARTH'S CONSPIRACY
WAKING US FROM HYPOCIRACY
IT'S THE MARCH OF TIMES
KEEPING TUNE OF NATURE'S RHYTHM

WATCHING THE SILHOUETTES OF SHADOWS DANCE

IT WAS AS IF WE COULD ALL JOIN HANDS

EVERYTHING ABOUT YOU IS MEMORIZED IN MY MIND

THE TRACING MAP OF FRECKLES DOWN YOUR SPINE

QUIETLY REASSURING MYSELF YOU'RE STILL MINE

WATCHING THE SILHOUETTES OF SHADOWS DANCE

IT WAS IF WE COULD JOIN HANDS

STRONG SCENT BURNED IN MY BRAIN

ROSEMARY..MINT

CLOUDED FROM A TEAR STAIN

STRETCHED AS FAR AS THE WAVES OF UNDERTOW

HOW DID I NOT SEE YOU YEARS AGO

AND NOT MOURN THE SLIVER OF A WINDOW

MISSION FADED AND FAITH LOW

WHAT DRAWS US BACK

I'LL WAIT FOR YOU

LIKE A LOVE SONG

LYRIC DEEP..SAD AND LONG

HOW DID I NOT SEE YOU YEARS AGO

STARING DEEP BOTH EYES COLOUR OF INDIGO

TWIST AND HOLD THAT ONE THREAD

WISHING FOR A LOVE STORY ONLY BURIED IN MY HEAD

WHEN I HEARD THAT SONG

MY HEART CALLED FOR YOU

I WANTED TO SING IT FULL AND LOUD

TO MIMIC HOW I FELT FOR YOU

AT THAT EXACT MOMENT

WHEN I KNEW WHAT LOVE WAS

STRICKEN LIKE A RUSH

SMELL OF SUMMER BRUSH

I STOOD IN THE MOMENT

LYRICS DREW TO AN END

I WANTED TO SING IT

FULL AND LOUD

I DON'T KNOW IF I CAN STAND TALL LIKE YOU

RISE FROM THE GRAIN

AMIDST ALL THIS PAIN

GRIND TO A SCREECHING HALT

GIVE IT ALL I GOT

I'M NOT STRONG LIKE YOU

RISE FROM THE ASH THE BURNING BRUSH

BLACK SMOKE CLOUDS MY SIGHT

NOT SURE I HAVE EVEN ONE MORE FIGHT

WE CAST JUDGEMENT ON OUR BROTHERS

BUT INSIDE IT'S ENVY THAT WE HIDE

I'M NOT STRONG LIKE YOU

I CRAWL IN THE DUST

WEEPING..GIVING INTO FAILURES LUST

IT'S INSTANTLY TEMPTING

I DON'T KNOW IF I CAN STAND TALL LIKE YOU

FIGHTING..LYING.. CHEATING..BITING..

THROW DOWN YOUR WEAPONS

YOUR SWORDS ..YOUR SHIELDS OF SHAME

SURRENDER YOUR MASKS ..YOUR ARMOUR..BLINDFOLDS

LOOK HIGH INTO THE SKY..INTO THE SUN

FOR LIGHT ..FOR LOVE..FOR STRENGTH

THE ANSWERS ARE WRITTEN IN THE SKY

ETCHED IN COLOURS DRAWN BY THE EARTH

BRING BACK STORIES OF STARY SKIES AND HEROIC TIES

TALES OF GOOSEBUMPS AND TEAR JERKING COMPASSION

SEE THE TOP OF THE MOUNTAINS AND PEOPLE WE COUNT ON

SMELL OF THE SILENT RAIN

AND THAT SHOULDER TO CRY ON

JUST BE STILL

THERE IS FRAGRANCE IN THE WIND

MUTING THE SOUND OF AN ANGRY SHRILL

BRING BACK STORIES OF COUNTLESS SUNSETS

AND THE TALE OF THE FIRST TIME WE MET

BRING BACK LAUGHTER..SOUND OF PEACE

BRING BACK STORIES OF STARY SKIES

AND GLIMMERS OF HOPE IN OUR LOVED ONE'S EYES

DRAW LINES AFTER THE FLAMES IN THE ASH

WRITE MY NAME

TATTOO ON MY BACK

BLOWN AWAY

GREY AND BLACK

I WROTE YOU OUT

AND WATCHED IT BURN

WE LOOK TOWARDS THE SHADOW OF STRANGERS

TO CAST UPON OUR RAGE

OUR ANGER

MY EYES ARE BURNT FROM THE DARK SMOKE

IT CLOUDS MY SIGHT

THEN MY SENSES AWOKE

THAT LURKS UP ONTO ME

LIGHT A MATCH

STENCH OF MIDNIGHT ECSTACY

HE WALKS CRIPPLED AND ALONE

NO LIGHT OF DAY ON HIS BROW HAS EVER SHONE

DRAG HEAVY BURDEN HIDDEN FROM THE NAKED EYE

SPIRALS OF REGRET WASH AWAY LIKE STAGNET WATER

DOWN THE DRAIN WITH THEM..WATCH THEM DIE

NIGHT SHADES TURN TO DAWN

FADING IN THE DISTANCE IS THE CRICKETS SONG

AFTER THE PARTY

AFTER THE CANDLES MELT

A HEARTFUL OF LOVE IS ALL I FELT

ECHO OF THE RECORD PLAYER AND IT'S LAST SONG

WE'VE BEEN APART FOREVER..WAY TOO LONG

AFTER THE PARTY

WHEN ALL THE GUESTS HAVE LEFT

OUR SECRET..OUR PROMISE I HAVE KEPT

AFTER THE PARTY

OUR LAST GOOD BYE

I'LL CRY ONE LAST TEAR AS YOU WIPE IT FROM MY EYE

IF YOU TAKE A SIP AND SEE WHERE IT GOES

HE'S THE HEALER NOONE KNOWS

THE MOON IS IN HALF PHASE

SIX DAYS IT WILL BE FULL

THE HEALER TAKES THAT SIP

I FEEL HIS ENERY PULL

BLOOD ON THE MOON

THE AIR IS THICK

WHERE IS THE HEALER

HE IS THE SAVIOUR I WILL PICK

CURSED MY DEMONS

WITH EACH CHANGING SEASON

CHANTED TO MY SOUL

I TURNED AWAY MY ANGELS

BURYING THEM DEEP IN A HOLE

THE HEALER TAKES THAT SIP

IM OBSESSED WITH THE SMELL ON HIS MOUTH

LET ME DRINK FROM HIS CUP OF PLENTY

HEAL AND BE FREE

UNTIL IT'S EMPTY

WHEN THE BLACK VEIL IS LAYERED OVER THE EARTH

IS WHEN I FEAR THE DARKNESS THE MOST

UNAPPRECIATED..UNAPOLOGETIC

CAST ASIDE YOUR LIES..MASKED WITHERED EYES

DAGGERS INSTEAD OF A SHIELD

WOUND OF BETRAYAL NEVER HEALED

CAST ASIDE YOUR TREASURES

THROW THEM TO THE WILD

THEY COME BACK CLEANSED

INNOCENT AS A CHILD

FALLEN FROM THE SKY

LIVE ANOTHER DAY BUT WISH TO DIE

CAST ASIDE YOUR PRIDE

BROKEN..BLIND

WASHED AWAY WITH THE OCEAN TIDE

CROUCH DOWN SHED NO TEAR

TURN A BLIND EYE FOR THE LAST DAY OF THE YEAR

CURSE OUT THE OLD

AFRAID OF THE NEW

STEP CAUTIOUSLY IN WHERE TIME IS DUE

KNELT DOWN I SHED NO TEAR

I HIDE MY HEAD FOR THE LAST DAY OF THE YEAR

I'LL FALL ON BENDED KNEE

FEEL YOUR HAND ON THE CROWN OF MY HEAD

AS YOU GAZE OVER ME

I'LL FALL DOWN TO WORSHIP AT YOUR ALTER

LOOK UP TO TO SHOW YOU THERE IS NO OTHER

MY HEALER..MY SPIRIT

I PRAY TO THY FATHER

HOLDING MY PRIDE

UNTIL I'M SHORT OF BREATH

I'LL LAY BY YOU

UNTIL MY DEATH

WE TELL STORIES OF OLD

GOLD LIGHT FLICKERS

PRETENDING WE ARE NOT COLD

WE SHIVER..WE FIGHT..WE CRY..WE DIE

CHAINED TO THE INSIDE

THE KEY WE CAN'T FIND

IT'S A THOUSAND SLEEPLESS NIGHTS

NEVER ESCAPING OUR MIND

WE SCREAM..WE FIGHT..WE CRY..WE FALL.. WE DIE

I FOUND YOU LOST ON WINTER'S DAWN

AS IF CAPTURED YOUR FATE WROTE A PRISONER'S SONG

MESSENGER..HIDDEN LETTER

LOOKING FOR WHAT WAS STOLEN

WOUNDED..SCARED

I TRACE ALL NIGHT

TO FIND YOU GRASPING ..FROZEN AT FIRST LIGHT

ARMS LAID OUT

HEART ON MY SLEEVE I REACH SO FAR

I STRUGGLE TO LEAVE

I LEFT YOU LOST ON WINTER'S DAWN

COME CLOSE LET ME WHISPER WITH WARM MOUTH

I TALK OF HATE AND DEMISE

I LOOK DEEPER PAST JUDGING EYES

BRING ME YOUR HATE

MY SERVENT OF BAD DEEDS

FOR MY REDEMPTION IS MUCH TOO LATE

SEE IT IN THE SIGNS OF STRANGERS

THEIR ILL HEALTH WORN OUT ANGER

COME CLOSE LET ME SCREAM

FOR AN EXISTENCE WE CAN ONLY DREAM

I REACH UP OUT OF THE FLAMES

MISGUIDED HOPE AND MISUNDERSTOOD LOVE

HEAD HELD HIGH I CAST YOU ASIDE

IT'S TOXIC

BROKEN HEART AND BRUISED LIMB

YOU SAID I'M NOT WORTHY..

WORTHY OF HIM

I REACH UP OUT OF THE FLAMES

DARK LIES DECEITFUL EYES

I HOLD MY HEAD HIGH AND CAST YOU ASIDE

WHEN THE TREE BRANCHED LOOK LIKE FINGERS TO THE SKY

IS WHEN I KNOW YOUR THOUGHTS ARE LIES

YOU HOLD THEM TIGHT TO YOUR CHEST

HOLDING SECURE DOING YOUR BEST

MASTER OF NOTHING FAILURE OF BLUFFING

I CAN'T FALL ASLEEP UNDER THE ASH SKY

I HOLD MY EYES AND STILL TRY

ALONE SURVIVING IN FEAR

EXHAUSTED YOUR FAKE TEAR

WHEN YOUR WEATHERED EYES LOOK TO THE SKY

IS WHEN I KNOW YOUR THOUGHTS ARE LIES

HEAVY HEART NEED TO GET THIS SICKNESS OFF MY CHEST

MALICE..STRESS

SWIMMING IN THE DEEP OF YOUR MESS

SO I REACH FOR THE ONE WHO RELEASED ME FROM THE FLAMES

THE ONE WITH DARK EYES

DUG UP FROM THE ASHES

HEALED ME FROM THE PAIN

IT WAS OLD FASHIONED TYPE WRITER ETCHED WORDS

SPELLED OUT IN INK OF A RIBBON

TATTOOED ON THE PAGE

FOREVER PRINTED FOR ALL TO SEE

CAREFULLY CRAFTED

POETICALLY VERSED

REFRESHING OPTIMISTIC

IN A WORLD OF COWARDLY TEXT MESSAGE

AND CYBER VERSE

HE SAVED HER

NOT WITH A SWORD OR SUIT OF ARMOUR

HE SAVED HER WITH KINDNESS AND PATIENCE

A HEALER NOT OF MEDICINE BUT WORDS

HOW HE COMPARED HER TO THE MOON

HE SAVED HER OVER AND OVER

EACH DAY FIGHTING HER BATTLES

HE SAVED HER

MIRRORS DAWN REFLECTION IS GONE

HOW DO YOU SILENCE THE MIND

WHEN THE BODY HAS LOST IT'S SONG

MAYBE FOR A MOMENT

YOU WILL ALWAYS BE MY FAVOURITE SEASON

MY ONE TRUE REASON

WALKING BENEATH THE LEAVES

SMELL THE OCEAN ON THE BREEZE

TUCKED AWAY FOR SAFE KEEPING

THROUGH THE YEARS YOU WERE SLEEPING

FAILED GRIEVING

THESE SEEM TO BE THE MOST OF FRAGILE DAYS

AS YOU WATCH THE SOULS AROUND YOU FADE AWAY

LACK OF CONTENT

CAN'T SIT STILL

BODY ILL

CROWN OF FIRE AROUND YOUR HEAD

LIKE A TARNISHED RING OF GOLD

SMOLDING EMBERS OF PRIDE OF MEMORIES OF OLD

I DIDN'T KNOW WHAT TO DO

DO WITH ALL THIS EMOTION

A TIDAL WAVE BENEATH MY SKIN

I HEARD THE VIOLINS START

THE WIND PICK UP

IT ALL EMERGING FROM THE OCEAN THE MOTION

SWEPT UP IN CASCADE OF WATER

I DIDN'T KNOW THAT IN LOVE

YOU GASP FOR AIR

REACH FOR THE SURFACE

DROWN IN THE CURRENT

I CAN'T RECALL THE TIME YOU WEREN'T IN MY LIFE

I SUSPECT THOUGH THE SUN WASN'T AS HOT

OR THE MOON SO BRIGHT

I WASN'T AS SURE OR AS BRAVE

TO LIFT MY WINGS AND SOAR WITH EASE

YOU FOUND ME STARING AT THE EARTH

QUESTIONING MY WORTH

A MILLION MILES TO FIND ME

MY EYES WET..MY MIND SET

WALKING WITH TIRED FEET

THEY LED YOU TO WHERE OUR EYES DID MEET

I'M NOT DESERVING OF THIS JOURNEY

I'M TOO MUCH DARKNESS

WRAPPED IN BRANCHES OF SADNESS

RIPPED FROM THE SEAMS LIKE A HURRICANE IN MY VEINS

WAKE ME FROM THIS VICIOUS DREAM

I'D RATHER BE BURIED ALIVE THEN WATCH MY HEART DIE LOVE'S DESIRE..HUNGER..FIRE

BITE MY NECK MAKE ME BLEED

THIS IS OUR LAST DANCE I'LL LET YOU LEAD

DEATH COMES IN CAREFULLY AND EASY
FOR THOSE THAT SPREAD LIGHT AND ASH ON THE WINDS
OF THE UNCHARTED..MISUNDERSTOOD
THE ONES RIDDLED WITH DISEASE OF THE MIND
DARKNESS COMES DOWN LIKE THE WARMING OF A POOL
THE LAYING DOWN IN A FIELD OF GRASS
WELCOMED..EMBRACED

LEAVE LOVE NOTES ETCHED ACROSS MY BODY

OF INTENTIONS AND DEMISE

GLIMPSES OF HELLFIRE IN YOUR EYES

MYSTERY MEETINGS

FRAGRANT LEAVINGS

I SEE THE EVIL IN THE SKY

A MILLION LIVES STRETCHED BEHIND OUR EYES

I HOLD TIGHT TO A PETAL

THE COLOUR OF SUNSHINE

IT'S THE LIGHT THAT BURSTS THROUGH DARKNESS

THAT MAKES ME STAND ALONE

BROKEN FIGHTING FOR THIS LAND

FLOWERS BLANKET IN BLACK

THE WIND BLOWS ENCOURAGING HOPE

IT'S THE LIGHT THAT BURSTS THROUGH DARKNESS

THAT MAKES ME STAND TOGETHER IN HEALING

FIGHTING FOR THIS LAND

IT'S WITH EARTH'S KISS AND HEAVEN'S EMBRACE

OUR LOVED ONES HAVE GONE TO THAT SPECIAL PLACE

THE BOND OF PARENT AND CHILD

BORN FREE AND EYES SO WILD

WE REMEMBER NEW STEPS

TEAR STAINED EYE

MISCHIEVOUS LAUGHTER AND LITTLE WHITE LIES

SPIRALED UP FROM THE SHORE

REBORN BEFORE THE DAWN

I EMERGE FROM THE FOG

BEAST BY MY SIDES

MY WOLVES WARN OF MY ARRIVAL

A SPECTUAL FIGURE

CAST IN DEVINE SPLENDOR

LOOKING FOR REVENGE

CRAVING THE TASTE OF DANGER

I SEE MY PREY

AND CRAWL NO FARTHER

STANDING TO CLOSE TO THE EDGE

I'M BORED..I'M RESTLESS

WHAT IF I REACH MY ARMS OUT AND TRY TO FLY

BUILT ON DOUBT LAYERS OF HURT

I'LL TRY TO DO BETTER.. SEE CLEARER

MY PROPOSAL TO DIG BENEATH THE SURFACE

REGAIN MY PURPOSE

THE MOON HAS A SECRET

IT WAS CASCADED ON THE FIREY REDS AND ORANGE OF THE SETTING SUN

NIGHT WILL SOON BE UPON US

INDIGO IN DARK SHADE

YOUR HEART WILL BE AT EASE

IT IS THE ONLY TIME YOU ARE UNDERSTOOD

AFTER A DEEP BREATH OF RELIEF

THE MOON HAS A SECRET

COME MEET ME WHERE THE STARS REFLECT IN THE DEEP DARK WATER

WE CAN BE AS ONE

WHERE NO EYES WILL SEE

IT'S THE ONLY TIME WHEN YOU ARE UNDERSTOOD

WHO WAS THAT MAN

STANDING IN THE DISTANCE

STERN BROW AND STERN STANCE

HIS STARE SOME WHAT FAMILIAR

HE STUDIED HER DANCE WITHIN THE FIELD

YOU COULD FIND HER THERE

HEART AS WILD AS HER HAIR

BRISKLY DANGLING IN HER EYES

LATE SEASON

WHEN THE DAYS BECOME SHORT...NIGHTS LONG

WHEN TWILIGHT BECOMES KING

GOLDEN HUES AND SPECKLED TREES

LOOKED LIKE DIAMONDS IN THE EYES OF SPECTATORS

AMBER AND AUBURN COVERED THE EARTH

WHO WAS THAT MAN

WITH AMUSED SMIRK AND EYES SO KIND

TAKING REFUGE IN A BLANKET OF AUTUMN FIELDS

A MYSTERY SO COMFORTING

AS HE STUDIED HER DANCE WITHIN THAT FIELD

TIRED OF PATIENCE WAITING TOO LONG

CHIMING IN THE NARRACISTIC TONES

LIKE HEARING DEATH'S SONG

DO YOU HOLD A TORCH FOR THEE

DO YOU LOVE ME

DROWN OUT THE SOUNDS OF INNER SCREAMS

I CAN'T SOLVE THIS MYSTERY

SMASHING MY FISTS

I FALL TOT HE GROUND

I COVER MY EARS

BUT I STILL HEAR THE SOUND

DO YOU HOLD A TORCH FOR THEE

DO YOU LOVE ME

TIED DOWN BY INVISIBLE ROPES

TETHERED TO THE EARTH

IS IT EVIL I HEAR

OR THE WIND CALLING OUT MY DEMONS

HEAVY IS THE BURDEN ON THIS BACK

NO SAVIOUR..ABSENT GOD

NO LOOKING BACK..EXILED

TO AN ISLAND TRAPPED IN MY HEAD

LET ME TAKE YOU DOWN

DROWN DEEP IN THE SCENT OF OCTOBER ON MY SKIN

WHISPERED FINGER ON YOUR LIP

PIN DROP

ARE YOU STILL THERE

I CANFEEL YOUR HEAT ON MY NECK

YOU TEETH ON MY FLESH

I SHY AWAY..BUT I'M NOT SCARED

I AM YOURS

REBORN IN THE SOIL

FORGOT WHAT WAS

NOTHING CAN GROW

I WAS BURIED BENEATH THE ROCK

DOWN DEEP AND LOW

WHERE CREATURES ROAM

JAGGED STONES AND ANCIENT BONES

I SEEK TO CATCH MY BREATH

I SEEK THE LIGHT

I AM YOURS

BRING ME TO THE SURFACE

WASH AWAY THE EARTH FROM MY BODY

AND BRING ME TO LIFE

WHO WAS IT YOU WERE WAITING FOR OUT ON THAT LIMB
WAS IT ME?

OR PERHAPS YOU WERE JUST SEEKING COMPANY
SLAM YOUR FIST

AGAINST THE KITCHEN TABLE

TRYING TO FILL THE VOID OF YOUR LONELY HEART YOU SEEK
REFUGE SOLELY AS AN ART

AFRAID OF THE NIGHT ALONE TWO MANY IN YOUR LIFE

MISCHIEVOUS PUPPETS IN SHADOWED LIGHT WAITING YEARS
FOR THT GIRL

YOU'D WAIT A THOUSAND MORE WAS IT ME?

OR WERE YOU JUST SEEKING COMPANY

THERE'S NO NEED TO THROW ME TO THE WOLVES

THEY COME WHEN I CALL

I AM THEIR EMPRESS, TEMPTRESS OF DARKNESS

JUDGE, EXECUTIONER

SENTENCED TO A FATE OF SIN

WASHED DOWN WITH A SHOT OF WHISKEY

JUST ENOUGH SO YOU DON'T MISS ME

THERE'S NO NEED TO THROW ME TO THE WOLVES

THEY COME FROM WHEN I CALL

THROUGH THE TREES, RHINESTONE CHAIN THEY LEAD

CURSES DRESSED AS A CURE

SENTENCED TO A FATE OF SIN

FEELING HOMETOWN

IT'S THE MEMORIES AT REST THAT PUT US TO THE TEST

LIGHT ON THE PORCH

SHADOW ON THE BARN

WHEN YOU HELD ME CLOSE

SAFE IN MY ARMS

IT'S THE TATTERED WHITE DRESS

MY HAIR SUCH A MESS

CASCADING GOLDEN HUES

ON THE DIRT ROAD, JUST YOU CAN ME

GOT LOST IN THE WIND

SO FAR OUT OF SIGHT

LOST MY DIRECTION

LOST YOU ON THAT GOLDEN LIGHT

DEDICATION

YOU ARE THE ONE WHO WOKE ME WHEN I REALIZED MY REALITY OF A BEAUTIFUL LIFE WAS FAR BETTER THAN MY DREAMS OF IT.

www.ingramcontent.com/pod-product-compliance
Lightning Source LLC
LaVergne TN
LVHW041543060526
838200LV00037B/1120